PHR/S

MW01108418

Aaron Frias, SPHR

This publication is designed to provide accurate and authoritative information regarding the subject matter covered. It is sold with the understanding that neither the publisher nor the author is engaged in rendering legal or other professional service. If legal advice or other expert assistance is required, the services of a competent, licensed professional should be sought. The federal and state laws discussed in this book are subject to frequent revision and interpretation by amendments or judicial revisions that may significantly affect employer or employee rights and obligations. Readers are encouraged to seek legal counsel regarding specific policies and practices in their organization.

ISBN 978-1468020977

Purpose of this Book

There are several books that cover the content you will need to familiarize yourself with the concepts and principals of Human Resource Management. Although this particular book does not include this type of course material, it does provide you with a way to measure and assess your preparedness for the PHR or SPHR certification exam.

The questions presented in this book may not necessarily be in the same format as the questions you will find on the actual exam. The methodology behind the practice test questions in this book is to measure the breadth and depth of your general HR knowledge. It is important to remember that obtaining a high score on this practice test is not indicative of how you will perform on the actual exam. This practice test should be used as a guide to help you identify where you need to focus your studies.

Another important note about the practice test is that the questions are presented in a specific order. The questions are grouped together by the main sections of the test. For example, the first questions cover Strategic Management. The next set of questions cover Workforce Planning and Employment. And so on. The actual exam will not be arranged in this fashion. On the actual exam, the questions will be presented in a random order.

Also note that this practice test has been designed for both PHR and SPHR candidates. The general body of knowledge is the same for both tests. The primary difference is the number of questions you will receive in each section. Several scenario-based questions are also included in this practice test to simulate similar questions you might see if you are taking the SPHR version of the exam.

The following functional areas are covered on this practice test:

- Strategic Management
- Workforce Planning and Employment
- Human Resource Development
- Total Rewards
- Employee and Labor Relations
- Risk Management
- Core Knowledge Required by HR Professionals

For additional information about the body of knowledge tested on the exam, how to apply to take the exam and what to expect on exam day, be sure to visit the official PHR/SPHR site: www.HRCI.org.

Note: This book and its author are not affiliated with HRCI or SHRM. The questions and answers in this practice test were not taken directly from the exam. The questions and explanation of answers were created based on the functional areas and body of knowledge set by HRCI. Passing or failing this practice exam does not guarantee a similar outcome on the actual exam.

For additional online practice tests, be sure to visit **www.PHRprep.com**.

Practice Test

1. Which of the following BEST shows a project's *critical path*?

    a. Work Breakdown Structure

    b. Pereto Chart

    c. PERT Chart

    d. GANNT Chart

2. Which of the following is an integral part of strategy development?

    a. Identifying threats and opportunities

    b. Taking corrective actions

    c. Determining low performers

    d. Measuring the overall performance of the organization

3. Which of the following is the largest HR-related professional organization in the world? It was originally founded as the American Society for Personnel Administration?

    a. ASPA

    b. HIPAA

    c. SHRM

    d. DOJ

4. Which of the following IS NOT a common role performed by the Human Resources department of a large organization?

    a. Employee Advocate

    b. Strategic

    c. Administrative

    d. Supply Chain

5. Which of the following operational terms refers to the ability to produce output?

    a. Scheduling

    b. Inventory

    c. Capacity

    d. Budget

6. This term describes a broad statement made by an organization that reflects their philosophy about a certain set of employee or management activities?

    a. A policy

    b. A vision statement

    c. A mission statement

    d. A task force

7. According to the Department of Labor's definition, which of the following IS NOT a characteristic of a profession?

    a. Recognition by the OFCCP

    b. A code of ethnics

    c. A defined body of knowledge

    d. Applied research to the field

8. An HR manager is assigning staff and allocating resources to a new benefits initiative that is being implemented. The HR manager is using which of the following management functions:

    a. Controlling

    b. Leading

    c. Planning

    d. Organizing

9. HRMS stands for?

    a. Human Resource Management Strategy

    b. Human Resource Management System

    c. HR Research Management System

    d. Human Resource Modernization Strategy

10. Which of the following terms BEST describes a large database storing HR and employee metrics?

    a. Intranet

    b. Data warehouse

    c. Application service provider

    d. Streaming video

11. The term "brand equity" refers to the:

    a. Value associated with a brand name

    b. Ability for a company to recruit candidates

    c. Propensity for a company to contribute to its community

    d. Capability of an organization to produce goods targeted at a specific demographic

12. This term refers to the action of postponing or canceling a bill?

    a. Vote

    b. Veto

    c. Quorum

    d. Policy

13. Which of the following approaches eliminates the need to set internal performance goals because it focuses on how the company performs against its peers?

    a. Internal approach

    b. Relative approach

    c. Goal-based approach

    d. SWOT analysis

14. Which of the following project management tools would BEST show the start and end times of a project?

    a. Organizational chart

    b. Six Sigma

    c. GANNT chart

    d. Pareto chart

15. A company is experiencing scheduling and backlog issues because it cannot keep up with the increasing demands of its customers. This is a characteristic of which stage of the organizational life cycle?

    a. Decline

    b. Introduction

    c. Growth

    d. Maturity

16. Roughly what percentage of the data will fall within -1/+1 Standard Deviations?

    a. 2/3
    b. 1/3
    c. 1/2
    d. 15/16

17. To ensure the availability and integrity of data within an HR database, the data should be:

    a. Wiped clean each year
    b. Accessible by all staff
    c. Backed up routinely
    d. Printed onto paper

18. Which of the following is NOT a common benefit found with implementing HR technologies?

    a. Increase in manual processes
    b. Improved automated processes
    c. Increase in productivity
    d. Reduction in duplicate data entry

19. Which of the following BEST fits into an organic organization?

    a. A bureaucracy

    b. An organization with high formalization

    c. A highly centralized organization with a narrow span of control

    d. A virtual organization

20. Which of the following is NOT a component of SWOT analysis?

    a. Strategies

    b. Weaknesses

    c. Opportunities

    d. Threats

21. As an HR manager, you need to compare your organization's turnover with other similar sized companies in your industry. Which of the following would be the BEST method to use?

    a. Forecasting

    b. Benchmarking

    c. SWOT Analysis

    d. Critical Path Analysis

22. Which of the following BEST describes a catalogue of the abilities and experiences of a company's workforce?

    a. Forced ranking

    b. Mission statement

    c. SWOT analysis

    d. Skills inventory

23. This term refers to the minimum number of members of an assembly that must be present to make a meeting valid?

    a. Quorum

    b. Policy

    c. Vote

    d. Veto

24. The following is equal to a company's liabilities plus their owners' equity?

    a. Debts

    b. Assets

    c. Profit

    d. Cash

25. Which of the following is not a typical characteristic of a project?

    a. Has objectives

    b. Has a project team

    c. Requires resources

    d. Is continual

26. In accounting, a balance sheet shows

   a. The organization's current ratio of debt

   b. Cash receipt and disbursement over a specific period of time

   c. A snapshot of a company's financial condition

   d. The profit or loss over a specific period of time

27. The CFO of your company wants you to put together a budget for the upcoming fiscal year starting from scratch. Which of the following budgeting methods does this BEST describe?

   a. Zero-based budgeting

   b. Incremental budgeting

   c. Formula budgeting

   d. Activity-based budgeting

28. The four components of marketing can be characterized using the four "P"s. Which of the following IS NOT one of the four "P"s of marketing?

   a. Place

   b. Product

   c. Pricing

   d. Profit

29. This term refers to the number of employees a manager directs?

    a. Centralization

    b. Span of control

    c. Matrix hierarchy

    d. Chain of command

30. As an HR manager, you want to evaluate the current effectiveness of your department. Which method BEST fits with your goal?

    a. SWOT analysis

    b. HR audit

    c. Cost-benefit analysis

    d. Return-on-investment analysis

31. All of the following are characteristics of a matrix structure EXCEPT:

    a. There are two supervisors

    b. The functional and divisional structures are joined

    c. Creates cross-functional support

    d. Improves unity of command

32. Which of the following BEST describes "analysis paralysis"?

    a. Too many analysts are hired for a project and the project runs out of financial resources

    b. There is not enough data to support a decision or to take action

    c. Data that is collected is too old and outdated so new data must be collected

    d. Data is collected and analyzed but a decision is not made and no action is taken

33. Which of the following is NOT considered a measure of central tendency?

    a. Correlation

    b. Mean

    c. Mode

    d. Median

34. What is the "Mean" of the following set of numbers: 1,1,3,3,5,5

    a. 2.5

    b. 3

    c. 3.5

    d. 5

35. If you have a large standard deviation, this means the data is:

    a. Bunched together

    b. Inaccurate

    c. Fairly diverse

    d. Unreliable

36. Research that utilizes open-ended questions BEST falls into which category?

    a. Deductive reasoning

    b. Inductive reasoning

    c. Quantitative analysis

    d. Qualitative analysis

37. The portion of baby boomers that is caring for both their children and their parents is known as the:

    a. Sandwich generation

    b. Generation X

    c. Generation Y

    d. Generation XY

38. Which of the following patent types BEST protects the invention of a new and useful manufacturing process?

    a. Design patent

    b. Plant patent

    c. Utility patent

    d. Copyright

39. An organization is using a forced ranking appraisal method to rate employees. This method ranks employees against:

    a. Their peers

    b. national benchmarks

    c. executives

    d. previous year's performance

40. Another term for the Ishikawa Chart is the:

    a. Critical path PERT chart

    b. Cause-and-effect diagram

    c. Scatter diagram

    d. Control chart

41. Which of the following is NOT considered a human process intervention?

    a. Leadership development

    b. Redesigning jobs

    c. Teambuilding exercises

    d. Conflict resolution

42. Which of the following should NOT be used in determining an objective?

    a. Measureable

    b. Vague

    c. Reasonable

    d. Timely

43. What is the first step in the scientific method?
    a. Hypothesis development
    b. Research design
    c. Data collection
    d. Problem identification

44. Which of the following will help you determine if a measurement actually measures something that cannot be directly observed?
    a. Construct validity
    b. Content validity
    c. Concurrent validity
    d. Predictive validity

45. Which of the following is true?
    a. If data is reliable, it must be valid
    b. If data is valid, it must be reliable
    c. If data is valid, it cannot be reliable
    d. If data is reliable, it cannot be valid

46. What is the mode of the following set of numbers (1,2,2,5,7,9,10)
    a. 2
    b. 5
    c. 7
    d. 10

47. What is the median of the following set of numbers (1,2,2,5,7,9,10)

    a. 2

    b. 5

    c. 7

    d. 10

48. Which of the follow percentages (approximated) reflect three standard deviations away from the mean?

    a. 50%

    b. 69%

    c. 95%

    d. 99%

49. If there is a negative correlation between two measures, which of the following is true?

    a. As the value of one measure decreases, the other measure increases

    b. As the value of one measure decreases, the other measure decreases

    c. As the value of one measure increases, the other measures increases

    d. As the value of one measure increases, the other measure's value does not change

50. Which of the following is NOT a component of an effective ethics program?

    a. Support from top-level, executive management

    b. Training on ethical behavior

    c. Code of ethics document

    d. All are components of an effective ethics program

51. Employers with less than this many employees are not covered by Title VII of the Civil Rights Act of 1964 (excluding state and local laws)?

    a. 500

    b. 100

    c. 15

    d. All companies are covered by the Civil Rights Act of 1964

52. Which agency enforces Affirmative Action?

    a. OFCCP

    b. DOJ

    c. DOL

    d. EEOC

53. The Age Discrimination in Employment Act (ADEA) protects the rights of individuals who are over this age?

    a. 16

    b. 18

    c. 40

    d. 65

54. Which of the following IS NOT specified in the Pregnancy Discrimination Act

    a. Pregnancy-related benefits are limited to married employees.

    b. If an employer provides any benefits to workers on leave, the employer must provide the same benefits for those on leave for pregnancy-related conditions.

    c. Employers must provide the same level of health benefits for spouses of male employees as they do for spouses of female employees.

    d. If an employee is temporarily unable to perform her job because of her pregnancy, the employer must treat her the same as any other temporarily disabled employee

55. An I-9 must be completed within this many hours of employment?

    a. 24

    b. 48

    c. 56

    d. 72

56. Under the Worker Adjustment and Retraining Notification (WARN) Act, an employer must notify its employees 60 days in advance of mass layoffs under all of the conditions EXCEPT:

    a. 55 full-time employees will be laid off in a company that has a total of 100 workers

    b. 550 full-time employees will be laid off

    c. 400 full-time, 100 part-time employees will be laid off

    d. 750 full-time employees will be laid off due to a natural disaster

57. Which of the following DOES NOT qualify as an individual with a disability under the ADA?

    a. Has a physical or mental impairment that substantially limits one or more major life activities

    b. Has a record of a physical or mental impairment that substantially limits one or more major life activities

    c. Is regarded as having a physical or mental impairment that substantially limits one or more major life activities

    d. Individuals currently engaging in the illegal use of drugs

58. Which of the following is not protected by Title VII of the Civil Rights Act

    a. Race

    b. Age

    c. Color

    d. Religion

59. Which of the following cases established the judicial concept of adverse impact?

    a. Griggs v. Duke Power

    b. McDonnell-Douglas Corp. v. Green

    c. Martin v. Wilks

    d. Harris v. Forklift Systems, Inc.

60. Which of the following is NOT true regarding "piecework"?

    a. It is a form of performance-related pay

    b. It does not provide an incentive for the employee to produce at a high level

    c. An employee is paid a fixed "piece rate" for each unit produced

    d. The output can be measured by the number of physical items produced

61. Which of the following cases established the judicial concept of disparate treatment?

    a. Griggs v. Duke Power

    b. McDonnell-Douglas Corp. v. Green

    c. Albermarle Paper v. Moody

    d. Washington v. Davis

62. An employee is suspected of being involved in a workplace incident of embezzlement which resulted in a considerable loss to your organization. Which of the following is TRUE?

    a. A polygraph test can be performed because the employee is a suspect and a loss was realized

    b. A polygraph can be performed on any employee regardless of suspicion when there is a loss

    c. A polygraph test cannot be conducted because there was a loss to the employer

    d. Polygraph tests can no longer be administered regardless of suspicion or loss

63. Which case established that employment tests and performance evaluations have to be job-related AND valid predictors of performance?

    a. McDonnell-Douglas Corp. v. Green

    b. Washington v. Davis

    c. Griggs v. Duke Power

    d. Albermarle Paper v. Moody

64. A bonus was given to all full-time employees. One full-time employee was out on FMLA during the time the bonuses were issued. The employer:

    a. Is not required to pay the employee the bonus when the return

    b. Is required to pay the employee at least half of the bonus when they return

    c. Has the option to pay or not pay the employee the bonus when they return

    d. Is required to pay the employee the bonus when they return

65. Which of the following is considered to be a comprehensive document covering the legality of employee selection procedures?

    a. SOX

    b. HIPAA

    c. UGESP

    d. ADEA

66. With regards to Affirmative Action, utilization analysis refers to:

    a. Analyzing the number of resources consumed by a project

    b. Comparing the availability analysis with the job group analysis

    c. The availability of a particular protected group in the organization

    d. The availability of a particular protected group in the community

67. Adverse impact occurs when the rate of selection for a protected class is less than THIS percent of the rate for the class with the highest selection rate?

    a. 20%

    b. 40%

    c. 60%

    d. 80%

68. As an HR manager you realize that adverse impact is occurring. Which of the following is NOT a choice for you as an employer?

    a. Abandon the procedure

    b. Validate the procedure as a business necessity

    c. Continue with the procedure

    d. Validate and confirm the job-relatedness of the procedure for the selection

69. Using the "two-factor analysis" for an affirmative action plan requires that a company evaluate these two factors?

    a. Total women and total minority populations

    b. Total minority population and job availability

    c. Job availability and the total women population

    d. Internal availability and external availability

70. All of the following are considered an immediate "family member" for purposes of taking FMLA leave EXCEPT?

    a. Employee's spouse

    b. Employee's mother-in-law

    c. Employee's son or daughter

    d. Employee's adopted son or daughter

71. An applicant assessment is inadvertently eliminating African-American applicants. Which of the following BEST describes what occurred?

    a. Adverse impact

    b. Disparate treatment

    c. Proper selection practice

    d. Glass ceiling

72. A verbal promise made between an employee and employer is called a:

    a. Grievance

    b. Express oral contract

    c. Injunction

    d. Arbitration

73. An employee arrives at work early and waits for their scheduled time of work to begin. According to the Portal-to-Portal Act:

    a. The time the employee was waiting is considered hour worked

    b. The Portal-to-Portal Act address termination procedures and does not helped explain or determine hours worked

    c. The time the employee was waiting is not considered hours worked

    d. The employee should be penalized time for showing up early

74. According to the Employee Commuting Flexibility Act of 1996, which of the following is TRUE?

    a. Commuting time is always paid work time regardless of the employee using a company vehicle or not

    b. Commuting time is paid work time only if the employee uses a company vehicle

    c. Commuting time is not paid work time if the employee uses a company vehicle but is if the employee is not using a company vehicle

    d. Commuting time is not paid work time regardless of the employee using a company vehicle or not

75. Which amendment to the Wage and Hour Law prohibits unequal pay for the equal or "substantially equal" work performed by both men and women?

    a. Equal Pay Act

    b. Portal-to-Portal Act

    c. Sarbanes-Oxley Act

    d. The Sherman Antitrust Act

76. According to the Equal Pay Act of 1963, which of the following is not considered in the determination of equal work factors?

    a. Effort

    b. Seniority

    c. Skills

    d. Working conditions

77. Which of the following IS NOT an Act that provides an opportunity for a tax credit by hiring certain individuals?

    a. Work Opportunity Tax Credit

    b. Welfare-to-work Tax Credit

    c. Worker Relocation Tax Credit

    d. Tax and Trade Relief Extension Act

78. Which of the following cases is most well-known for setting the precedent for reverse discrimination?

  a. City of Richmond v. J.A. Croson Company

  b. Regent of the University of California v. Bakke

  c. Harris v. Forklift Systems, Inc.

  d. Ellerth v. Burlington Northern

79. An employee is approached by their director who promises the employee a promotion in return for sexual favors. This is an example of:

  a. Quid pro quo

  b. Carpe diem

  c. Caveat emptor

  d. Per diem

80. Which of the following terms refers to a situation where the advancement of a qualified person to a higher level in the organization from a lower level is prevented based on their gender?

  a. Price floor

  b. Brick floor

  c. Glass ceiling

  d. Price ceiling

81. Based on the common sequence of events the EEOC takes when they receive a compliant of discrimination, which of the following steps would occur first?

    a. The EEOC issues a Letter of Determination

    b. The EEOC issues a right-to-sue letter

    c. The EEOC determines if it has jurisdiction over the complaint filed

    d. The EEOC files suit against the employer

82. Of the following techniques for forecasting workforce needs, which one requires that the participants not meet face-to-face?

    a. Ratio analysis

    b. Trend analysis

    c. Nominal group technique

    d. Delphi technique

83. As an HR manager, you are tracking which employees are currently ready for a promotion into specific, key positions. Which of the following terms BEST describes this process?

    a. Succession planning

    b. Replacement charting

    c. SWOT analysis

    d. Critical path method

84. You need to collect data for your company's job analysis needs. Your company has a large number of employees that occupy the same job and they are spread out over a wide geographic area. Which of the follow data collection methods is the MOST appropriate?

    a. Questionnaires and checklists

    b. Observation

    c. Work sampling

    d. Interviews

85. Which of the following sections of the job description would a description about the environmental conditions such as weather, fumes, heat or cold, noise, etc. be found on?

    a. Job summary

    b. Essential functions

    c. Working conditions

    d. Qualifications

86. Which of the following would LEAST likely be an advantage of internal hiring versus external hiring?

    a. Brings new ideas into the workplace

    b. Reduces recruiting expenses

    c. Promote high morale

    d. Provides a career path for employees

87. Due to the potentially high cost and expenses involved, this applicant testing solution is typically reserved for higher-level positions:

    a. Cognitive ability tests

    b. Physical ability tests

    c. Personality tests

    d. Assessment center tests

88. When unemployment levels are low, which of the following would MOST likely be true?

    a. Recruitment is more difficult

    b. Employee retention is higher

    c. Workplace injuries decrease

    d. Employee satisfaction is higher

89. While interviewing a potential candidate for a job opening, a recruiter asks the candidate how they would handle a particular scenario. This is an example of a(n):

    a. Stress interview

    b. Structured interview

    c. Situational interview

    d. Informal interview

90. Which of the following executive orders prohibited employment discrimination on the basis of race, creed, color or national origin?

    a. EO 11375

    b. EO 11478

    c. EO 11246

    d. EO 11333

91. Which of the following questions could be asked during an interview?

    a. How many children do you have?

    b. Have you been arrested?

    c. Do you have a disability?

    d. Have you worked at this company before?

92. According to the Fair Labor Standards Act, what is minimum amount of time you should retain payroll records?

    a. 1 year

    b. 2 years

    c. 3 years

    d. 5 years

93. Which of the following is not a determination of *fair use* with regards to copyright laws?

  a. The purpose and character of the use, including whether such use is of a commercial nature or is for nonprofit educational purposes

  b. The nature of the copyrighted work

  c. Whether permission was obtained from the copyright owner

  d. The effect of the use upon the potential market for or value of the copyrighted work

94. Which term is used to describe how adults learn?

  a. pedagogy

  b. andragogy

  c. oligopoly

  d. flashogoy

95. You have an employee that learns best by listening to an instructor in a lecture setting. Which learning style is demonstrated?

  a. Visual

  b. Auditory

  c. Psychomotor

  d. Kinesthetic

96. Which of the following learning levels demonstrates the highest level of learning achieved?

    a. Synthesis

    b. Analysis

    c. Comprehension

    d. Knowledge

97. Which of the following DOES NOT belong on the hierarchy of needs as defined by Abraham Maslow?

    a. Self-actualization

    b. Social

    c. Esteem

    d. Motivation

98. According to Theory X and Theory Y, which of the following DOES not belong in Theory X?

    a. Human beings are lazy and dislike work

    b. Employees want to be directed

    c. Employees are self-motivated

    d. Employees value security above other factors associated with the workplace

99. Which of the following is a characteristic of the Herzberg's Two-Factor Theory?

    a. Hygiene

    b. Social

    c. Esteem

    d. Safety

100. Which of the following is not a component of Lewin's organizational change model?

    a. Unfreezing

    b. Freezing

    c. Movement

    d. Culture

101. Which of the following theories has the strongest linkage between compensation and performance?

    a. Goal-setting theory

    b. Expectancy theory

    c. Herzberg's two-factor theory

    d. McClelland's theory of needs

102. An employee seems to learn the most from PowerPoint presentations. Which of the following learning styles BEST fits with this statement?

    a. Auditory

    b. Kinesthetic

    c. Psychomotor

    d. Visual

103. Which of the following terms is not included in the HRD process acronym ADDIE?

    a. Needs Assessment

    b. Program Development

    c. Program Initiation

    d. Program Evaluation

104. Classroom participants are asked to pretend to be in specific roles to act out how their characters would respond in imaginary situations. What type of delivery method is demonstrated?

    a. Case Study

    b. Lecture

    c. Group discussion

    d. Role-playing

105. You are facilitating a large group through a leadership development workshop. The workshop requires a lot of small group breakouts and small group activities. Which room arrangement would BEST accommodate this need?

    a. Banquet

    b. Classroom

    c. V-Shape

    d. Rectangle

106. Which of the following HR interventions aligns individuals with the company's goals and measures the successful attainment of those goals?

    a. Management by Objectives (MBO)

    b. Coaching

    c. Team Building

    d. Career Planning

107. An employee copies an entire document posted on the IRS web page during a lecture on deferred compensation tax rules. Which of the following is TRUE?

    a. The employee violated copyright protections of the document because they did not have expressed permission to recreate and distribute the information

    b. The employee did not violate any copyright protections of the document because government documents are considered public domain

    c. The employee did not violate any copyright protections of the document because government documents are considered imminent domain

    d. The employee violated the copyright protections of the document because they copied and distributed copyright protected material

108. Which of the following IS NOT one of Kirkpatrick's four levels of evaluation?

    a. Reception

    b. Learning

    c. Behavior

    d. Results

109. A manager is great at leading employees towards meeting organizational goals through clear work guidelines and straight forward performance expectations. The manager also ensures that work is complete efficiently. Which of the following leadership types would BEST describe this type of manager?

    a. Transformational leadership

    b. Charismatic leadership

    c. Visionary leadership

    d. Transactional leadership

110. Which of the following IS NOT a "driving" force of change?

    a. New management

    b. New federal regulations

    c. Change in technology

    d. Tradition

111. An employee has taken something he learned from training and applied it on the job which in turn improved her performance at the task. Which level of Kirkpatrick's four levels has the employee achieved?

    a. Learning

    b. Analysis

    c. Synthesis

    d. Behavior

112.   Which of the following charts is a graphical representation of the 80/20 rule?

a.   Histogram

b.   Pareto

c.   GANTT

d.   PERT

113.   Which of the following career development programs allows an employee to choose between pursuing a management role or a technical expert role?

a.   Matrix

b.   Dual career ladder

c.   Job bidding

d.   Succession plan

114.   An executive has the ability to articulate his vision and inspire and evoke strong emotion in the employees to follow that vision. Which leadership type is being displayed?

a.   Transactional

b.   Transformational

c.   Charismatic

d.   Visionary

115. Which of the following IS NOT a characteristic of a learning organization?

    a. Systems-thinking

    b. Individual level training

    c. Personal mastery

    d. Mental models

116. Which of the following is not a type of training evaluation?

    a. Ranking

    b. Learning

    c. Behavior

    d. Results

117. What is the first step in conducting a training needs analysis?

    a. Identification of the performance gap

    b. Estimate the budget impact

    c. Recommend solutions

    d. Conduct training

118. Based on the managerial grid developed by Blake and Mouton that depicts managerial style based on concern for people and concern for production, which cell is the most favorable to be in?

    a. 1,9

    b. 9,1

    c. 1,1

    d. 9,9

119. Which of the following IS NOT an advantage of peer-team ratings?

    a. Peers have a significant amount of close contact with the employee

    b. Helpful when the leader does not have a close proximity or contact with the employee

    c. Employee's peers may give higher or lower rating based on non-work related items

    d. Manager may not have the expertise to properly evaluate the employee's performance that peers may have

120. An employee's performance rating is low because the manager based the employee's performance on the poor performance of the employee's peers. This is an example of:

    a. The horn effect

    b. The halo effect

    c. Recency

    d. Contrast error

121. Which of the following acts does not have a direct relation to the compensation and benefits of a company's employees?

    a. Uniform Guidelines on Employee Selection Procedures

    b. Fair Labor Standards Act

    c. Portal-to-portal Act

    d. Equal Pay Act

122. FLSA covers all of the following except:

    a. Overtime

    b. Paid Time Off

    c. Minimum Wage

    d. Minimum Age of Workers

123. How many weeks of unpaid medical leave does FMLA provide?

    a. 4

    b. 12

    c. 26

    d. 52

124. Under FMLA, if the leave can be reasonably anticipated, how many notice must the employee give the employer?

    a. 7 days

    b. 14 days

    c. 30 days

    d. 90 days

125. Which Act prohibits firms from deducting compensation in excess of one million dollars for its top five executives as a business expense unless the compensation is based on performance?

    a. Sarbanes-Oxley Act

    b. Health Insurance Portability and Accountability Act

    c. Taxpayer Relief Act

    d. Omnibus Budget Reconciliation Act

126. You could use the IRS 20-Factor Test to determine?

    a. If an employee is exempt

    b. Whether someone is an employee or an independent contractor

    c. If an employee is non-exempt

    d. If the employee's compensation is tax deductable

127. Which of the following job evaluation methods does the paired comparison method belong to?

    a. Ranking

    b. Job classification

    c. Point factor

    d. Factor comparison

128. Which of the following job evaluation methods uses compensable factors and external job market benchmarks?

    a. Ranking

    b. Job classification

    c. Point factor

    d. Factor comparison

129. Which of the following terms refers to collapsing multiple pay grades into one pay grade that has a wide range?

    a. Golden parachute

    b. Broad-banding

    c. Red circle rate

    d. Green circle rate

130. Which of the following is MOST LIKELY to happen when comparable external job market pay rates rise faster than similar internal job pay rates?

    a. Broad-banding

    b. Wide-banding

    c. Pay compression

    d. Green circle rates

131. An employee's pay rate has been frozen from future merit increases because their pay rate is higher than the maximum of their pay grade. This was likely caused by which of the following?

    a. Red circle rate was identified

    b. Green circle rate was identified

    c. Yellow circle rate was identified

    d. Black circle rate was identified

132. This Act requires the administrator of an employee benefit plan to furnish participants and beneficiaries with a summary plan description (SPD), clearly describing their rights, benefits, and responsibilities under the plan?

    a. Health Insurance Portability and Accountability Act (HIPAA)

    b. Consolidated Omnibus Budget Reconciliation Act (COBRA)

    c. Employee Retirement Income Security Act (ERISA)

    d. Family and Medical Leave Act (FMLA)

133. An employee earns more when they produce more. Which term BEST fits with this model?

    a. Piece rate plan

    b. Standard hour plan

    c. Flat rate plan

    d. Green circle plan

134. Which of the following IS NOT a pay differential?

    a. Hazard pay

    b. Shift pay

    c. Base pay

    d. Overtime

135. Which of the following in NOT an advantage of organization-wide incentives?

    a. Potential to increase employee retention

    b. Rewards all employees for meeting company-wide targets

    c. Recognizes superior individual performance

    d. Might have tax benefits for the organization

136. A golden parachute is a(n)

    a. Generous severance plan for executives

    b. Type of sign-on bonus for executives

    c. Annual bonus given to executives for high performance

    d. Guaranteed bonus for employees given on a quarterly basis

137. An employee feels satisfaction for completing a challenging project. Which of the following BEST describes the type of reward this employee received?

   a. Extrinsic reward

   b. Intrinsic reward

   c. Total reward

   d. Compensatory reward

138. What does KSA generally refer to?

   a. Knowledge, strategy and Analysis

   b. Kindness, satisfaction and acknowledgment

   c. Knowledge, skills and abilities

   d. Know-how, strategy and analysis

139. What does QDRO stand for?

   a. Qualified Domestic Relations Orders

   b. Qualified Disability Recipient Order

   c. Qualified Disaster Recovery Officer

   d. Qualified Disability Recruitment Officer

140. Which of the following federal laws does not directly apply to cash balance pension plans?

   a. Age Discrimination in Employment Act (ADEA)

   b. Employee Retirement Income Security Act (ERISA)

   c. Fair Labor Standards Act (FLSA)

   d. Internal Revenue Code (IRC)

141.   Which act protects an employee from being terminated solely based on the fact that their wages are being garnished for one debt?

   a.   Family Medical Leave Act (FMLA)

   b.   Fair Labor Standards Act (FLSA)

   c.   Health Insurance Portability and Accountability Act (HIPAA)

   d.   Consumer Credit Protection Act (CCPA)

142.   A job requires at least 2 years of project management experience and a bachelor's degree in business, MIS or the equivalent. These are examples of:

   a.   Essential job functions

   b.   Competencies

   c.   Job specifications

   d.   Job enrichment

143.   Which of the following is an immigrant visa?

   a.   B-1

   b.   L-1

   c.   EB-1

   d.   H-1B

144. Which of the following would not commonly be associated as a 'perk' for an executive?

   a. Club memberships

   b. Non-exempt status

   c. Low-interest loans

   d. Use of corporate vehicles

145. Which of the following is NOT a legislatively mandated benefit?

   a. Social security

   b. Workers' compensation

   c. Unemployment compensation

   d. Bereavement

146. Of the following types of health insurance, which offers the MOST flexibility when selecting health care providers?

   a. Health maintenance Organizations

   b. Preferred provider organizations

   c. Fee-for-service plans

   d. Employer funded health insurance

147.   Your organization is trying to improve the work/life balance of its employees. Which of the following programs will have the LEAST impact on that initiative?

    a. Offering a robust severance package

    b. Having an employee concierge service

    c. Providing onsite child care services

    d. Allow for flex scheduling

148.   Which of the following provide pretax health insurance possibilities for the employee?

    a. Section 125

    b. Section 150

    c. Section 225

    d. Section 529

149.   If funds in a flexible spending account are not used, what happens to the funds?

    a. The organization must return the funds to the employee

    b. The employee forfeits any unspent funds

    c. The government issues a check to the employee for the difference

    d. The funds rollover to the next year

150. An employee is currently making $10/hour. The minimum of the employee's pay grade is $5 and the maximum is $15. What is the comp-ratio?

    a. 0

    b. 1

    c. 5

    d. 10

151. The NLRB v. Jones and Laughlin established

    a. That the Wagner act was constitutional

    b. That the Wagner act was unconstitutional

    c. That yellow-dog contract illegal

    d. That the Taft-Hartley act was constitutional

152. Which of the following was one of the first national unions?

    a. American Federation of Labor

    b. National Labor Party

    c. Citizen for Organized Labor

    d. Knights of the Old Republic

153. A manager creates an environment for the employee that is hostile and inhospitable in an attempt to force the employee to resign. This is an example of

   a. Defamation

   b. Constructive discharge

   c. Slander

   d. Libel

154. Which of the following IS NOT a mandatory benefit?

   a. Social Security

   b. COBRA

   c. FMLA leave

   d. Paid time off

155. Which of the following is used to determine current market trends in setting pay levels that lead, meet, or lag the market?

   a. HAY system

   b. SWOT analysis

   c. Salary survey

   d. Compa-ratio

156. As of July 24, 2009, the federal minimum wage is

    a. $5.15

    b. $5.65

    c. $7.15

    d. $7.25

157. Which act establishes minimum wage?

    a. Family Medical Leave Act

    b. Portal-to-portal act

    c. Fair Labor Standards Act

    d. Wagner Act

158. A 15-year old works at a hospital part-time. Which of the following is a violation of the Fair Labor and Standards Act?

    a. The teen works outside of school hours

    b. The teen works 32 hours per week during non-school weeks

    c. The teen works 20 hours per week when school is in session

    d. The teen works a maximum of 6 hours a day during non-school weeks

159. Which of the following employer actions is legal to perform during a unionization drive?

    a. Issuing a statement to all employees that the company is not in favor of being unionized.

    b. Giving everyone a raise before the vote

    c. Forcing an employee to share their thoughts about the union

    d. Threatening to terminate the employee for saying encouraging things about the union

160. An employee agrees not to become a member of a union as a condition of employment. This is an example of

    a. Double-breasting

    b. A yellow-dog contract

    c. Salting

    d. A zipper clause

161. This act outlawed yellow-dog contracts?

    a. Norris-LaGuardia Act

    b. Wagner Act

    c. Taft-Hartley Act

    d. HIPAA

162. A union has one of its members apply to work for an organization in an attempt to organize that company's employees into their union. This is an example of

    a. Salting

    b. Double-breasting

    c. Sympathy picket

    d. A yellow-dog contract

163. The Landrum-Griffin Act is also known as which of the following?

    a. NLRB

    b. Federal Anti-Injunction Act

    c. Clayton Act

    d. Labor Management Reporting and Disclosure Act

164. Which of the following is a register of names and addresses of employees who are eligible to vote in a union certification election?

    a. Consent Election List

    b. Union certification Register

    c. Weingarten List

    d. Excelsior List

165. Which of the following Supreme Court decisions determined that compulsory arbitration as a condition of employment was legal?

    a. Roe v. Wade

    b. Circuit City v. Adams

    c. Griggs v. Duke Power

    d. McDonnell-Douglas Corp. v. Green

166. Which of the following groups is permitted into a bargaining unit?

    a. Confidential employees

    b. Managers

    c. Employees

    d. Supervisors

167. Which of the following is a permissible activity that a union can engage in?

    a. Salting

    b. Yellow-dog Contracts

    c. Engaging in a ULP

    d. Threatening employees

168. According to the acronym TIPS, an employer cannot do any of the following except?

    a. Threaten an employee

    b. Interrogate employees

    c. Promise employees better benefits

    d. Put a non-solicitation policy in place

169.   A petition by employees to "decertify" a union must be signed by what percentage of the bargaining unit?

   a.   10%

   b.   25%

   c.   30%

   d.   51%

170.   Which of the following is not a mandatory bargaining item?

   a.   Regular wages

   b.   Shift differential pay

   c.   Seniority

   d.   Paid time off

171. Both parties agree to include shift differential pay as a bargaining item in the collective bargaining process. This is an example of a(n)

   a.   Permissive bargaining item

   b.   Illegal bargaining item

   c.   ULP

   d.   Mandatory bargaining item

172. An employer insists on a closed shop to the union during the collective bargaining session. This is an example of a(n)

    a. Illegal bargaining item

    b. Mandatory bargaining item

    c. Permissive bargaining item

    d. Distributive bargaining item

173. The NLRB will hold an election if this percentage of authorization cards have been signed by the bargaining unit?

    a. 25%

    b. 30%

    c. 50%

    d. 60%

174. The NLRA prohibits a union from having an election because there was an election within 12-months of the proposed election. This is an example of a(n)

    a. Contract bar

    b. Blocking-charge bar

    c. Prior-petition bar

    d. Statutory bar

175. If a union petitioning for an election withdraws the petition before the election, they must wait this number of months before they can hold another election?

    a. 6 months

    b. 10 months

    c. 12 months

    d. 24 months

176. Which clause requires all employees to join the union or pay union dues regardless of their intent to join the union?

    a. Agency shop

    b. Closed shop

    c. Union shop

    d. Open shop

177. Which of the following clauses is illegal?

    a. Agency shop

    b. Closed shop

    c. Union shop

    d. Open shop

178. Which of the following is implemented to help prevent the reopening of collective bargaining negotiations during the term of the contract?

    a. Close shop clause

    b. Agency clause

    c. Zipper clause

    d. Dues check-off clause

179. Which of the following terms describes a temporary work-stoppage initiated by a company's employees?

    a. Strike

    b. Closed Shop

    c. FMLA

    d. Boycott

180. Which of the following is not a common bargaining tactic?

    a. Boycott

    b. Picketing

    c. Economic strike

    d. Closed shop

181. A union gets several customers of a company begin to file complaints against the company like the EEOC, OSHA and the Department of Labor. Which bargaining tactic BEST describes this scenario?

    a. Agency shop

    b. Picket line

    c. Corporate campaign

    d. Boycott

182. A company is bargaining with a union. The employees are picketing the primary company. The company has a subsidiary company that is non-union. The employees are picketing that company as well. The company can be described as being:

    a. Agency shop

    b. Closed shop

    c. Double breasted

    d. Common situs

183. Which of the following definitions describe when picketing by a labor union of an entire construction project is a result of a grievance held against a single subcontractor on the project?

    a. Common situs

    b. Double breasting

    c. Boycotting

    d. Corporate picketing

184. Which of the following is a tactic taken by a company's management during the bargaining process?

    a. Economic strike

    b. Lockout

    c. Work slowdown

    d. Corporate campaign

185. Impasse describes

    a. When future bargaining will not likely result in an agreement

    b. When a union refuses to continue bargaining negotiations

    c. When an employer refuses to continue bargaining negotiations

    d. When the NLRA forces both parties to continue bargaining

186. Which of the following IS NOT a common contract provision?

    a. Union security

    b. Grievance procedure

    c. No strike clause

    d. Agency shop

187. Which of the following is not commonly found on a three-person arbitration panel?

   a. An arbitrator selected by the company

   b. An arbitrator selected by the union

   c. An arbitrator selected by the government

   d. A neutral arbitrator

188. Employees start a strike without the knowledge of the labor union while a labor agreement is in place? This is an example of a:

   a. Sympathy strike

   b. Wildcat strike

   c. Economic strike

   d. Recognition strike

189. A strike is conducted in support of other striking unions. This is also known as a:

   a. Sympathy strike

   b. Economic strike

   c. Wildcat strike

   d. Recognition strike

190. What is the last step in the NLRB ULP compliant process?

   a. Initiation

   b. Investigation

   c. Hearing

   d. Appeal/Enforcement

191. Which group has authority over unfair labor practices for federal employees?

    a. National Labor Relations Board (NLRB)

    b. National Mediation Board (NMB)

    c. North American Free Trade Agreement (NAFTA)

    d. Federal Labor Relations Authority (FLRA)

192. Which of the following is a binding agreement regarding trade between the United States, Mexico and Canada?

    a. NAFTA

    b. WTO

    c. FMLA

    d. HIPAA

193. Which law allows an employee or employer to terminate the employment relationship at any time for any reason?

    a. Portal-to-portal Act

    b. Family Medical Leave Act

    c. Employment-at-will

    d. No strike clause

194. Which of the following IS NOT a tort?

    a. Defamation

    b. Employment contract

    c. Wrongful termination

    d. Negligent hiring

195. What is the final step of the progressive disciplinary process?

    a. Written warning

    b. Verbal warning

    c. 2nd written warning

    d. Termination

196. Which of the following describes a person who acts as a trusted intermediary between an organization and some internal or external constituency while representing the broad scope of constituent interests?

    a. Mediator

    b. Ombudsman

    c. Arbitrator

    d. Peer Review Panel Coordinator

197. If a process has many of its unnecessary steps removed, it is known to be:

    a. Lean

    b. Fat

    c. Cleansed

    d. Scrubbed

198. If a union loses a representation election, when is the soonest they can hold another election?

    a. Immediately

    b. 6 months

    c. 12 months

    d. 24 months

199. Which of the following BEST describes an Act that helped to control business monopolies?

    a. Sherman Antitrust Act

    b. Railway Labor Act

    c. Portal-to-portal Act

    d. Patent Act

200. Which Act limited the use of injunctions to break strikes?

    a. Railway Labor Act

    b. Clayton Act

    c. Wagner Act

    d. Labor-Relations Relations Act

201. Union members have made an agreement not to handle goods made by another non-union plant. This is an example of a(n):

    a. Featherbedding

    b. Zipper clause

    c. Hot-cargo clause

    d. Secondary boycott

202. Which Act established the Occupational Safety and Health Administration (OSHA)?

    a. Fair Labor Standards Act

    b. Occupational Safety and Health Act

    c. Family Medical Leave Act

    d. Taft-Hartley Act

203. Which OSHA standard requires a company to communicate, inventory, and evaluate chemical hazards in the workplace?

    a. Means of Egress standard

    b. Hearing Conservation standard

    c. Control of Hazardous Energy standard

    d. Employee Right-to-Know law

204. You will find the MSDS at many companies to assist in staying compliant with the OSHA Hazard Communication standard. What does MSDS stand for?

    a. Material Safety Data Sheets

    b. Manual System Directive Scenarios

    c. Manual System Data Simulations

    d. Mandatory Statistical Dynamic Situations

205. Which term refers to incorporating locks, disconnection switches, and shutoff valves to ensure equipment cannot be turned on?

    a. Tagout

    b. Lockout

    c. Logoff

    d. Tripswitch

206. An employee puts a sign on a machine to let other employee know not to turn it on while the employee is working on it. This is commonly referred to as:

    a. Lockout

    b. Login

    c. Tagout

    d. Egress

207. The Needlestick Safety and Prevention Act revised this OSHA standard?

    a. Personal Protective Equipment standard

    b. Confined Space Entry standard

    c. Hazardous Communication standard

    d. Bloodborne Pathogens standard

208. Which of the following rules absolves employers of responsibility if a coworker's actions cause an injury?

   a. Fellow servant rule

   b. 80-20 rule

   c. Means of egress

   d. Fair Labor Standards Act

209. Which of the following is not one of the common law doctrines that apply to worker's compensation or workplace injuries?

   a. Fellow servant rule

   b. Doctrine of contributory negligence

   c. The general duty standard

   d. Voluntary assumption of risk

210. Except for low-hazard organizations, businesses with more than this many employees must report all employee occupational injury and illness data?

   a. 5

   b. 10

   c. 25

   d. 50

211. Which of the following DO NOT apply to permit-required confined spaces as covered by the OSHA Confined Space Entry standard?

    a. MSDS documentation is provided to employees

    b. Training to be completed before an employee can enter the permit-required confined space

    c. A written safe-entry program reviewed by employees and OSHA officials

    d. Entry controls like permits, observers and entry supervisors

212. Which of the following would not require an employer to report a work-related injury to OSHA?

    a. Death

    b. Days away from work

    c. First aid-treatment

    d. Loss of consciousness

213. Which of the following is used to classify work-related injuries and illnesses and to note the extent and severity of each case?

    a. OSHA Form 100

    b. OSHA Form 300A

    c. OSHA Form 301

    d. OSHA Form 300

214. Which OSHA form would you use to show the total work-related injuries and illnesses for the year?

    a. OSHA Form 100

    b. OSHA Form 300A

    c. OSHA Form 300

    d. OSHA Form 301

215. OSHA Form 301, the injury and illness incident report, must be completed within how many days after you learn about a work –related injury or illness?

    a. 3 days

    b. 7 days

    c. 14 days

    d. 30 days

216. A common benchmark now used in place of tracking lost workdays is DART. What does DART stand for?

    a. Disability, aggravation, restrictions and transfers

    b. Days away, restricted or transferred

    c. Disability analysis of recurring traumas

    d. Dynamic aggregation rate tabulation

217. An OSHA compliance and safety officer must give an employer this many days notice before appearing on site?

    a. No notice

    b. 24 hours

    c. 48 hours

    d. 72 hours

218. An employer has the right to all of the following EXCEPT for:

    a. Request and receive proper identification from the OSHA officer

    b. Accompany the compliance officer on the inspection

    c. Refuse an inspection and require a search warrant

    d. Be given 48 hours notice before the compliance officer can perform the inspection

219. A violation is cited that has no direct or immediate relationship to job safety or health. This would be considered what type of violation?

    a. Repeat

    b. De Minimis

    c. Other-than-serious

    d. Serious

220. An employer places chains with padlocks around key exit doors in the building. This would MOST LIKELY be classified as which type of OSHA violation?

    a. De Minimis

    b. Other-than-serious

    c. Serious

    d. Willful

221. How long must an employer post an OSHA citation at or near the area the violation occurred?

    a. One day or until the violation is corrected, whichever is longer

    b. Two days or until the violation is corrected, whichever is longer

    c. Seven days or until the violation is corrected, whichever is longer

    d. Three days or until the violation is corrected, whichever is longer

222. Which of the following IS NOT a common risk factor for musculoskeletal disorder?

    a. Frequent repetitions

    b. Heavy lifting

    c. Excessive pressure

    d. Awkward positions

223. An employee fails to wear the proper gloves when handling a chemical and gets burned. This is an example of:

    a. An unsafe condition

    b. An unrecognized hazard

    c. An unsafe act

    d. A willful violation

224. Which of the following organizations should employers contact for information about substances used in work processes to determine whether or not they are toxic?

    a. National Institute for Occupational Safety and Health

    b. Department of Labor

    c. Office of Federal Contract Compliance Programs

    d. Department of Justice

225. An employer intentionally and knowingly violates an OSHA standard and receives a $70,000. Which level of citation did the employer likely receive?

    a. Repeat

    b. Willful

    c. Serious

    d. Failure to Abate

Practice Test Answer Key

1.	C	22.	D	43.	D
2.	A	23.	A	44.	A
3.	C	24.	B	45.	B
4.	D	25.	D	46.	A
5.	C	26.	C	47.	B
6.	A	27.	A	48.	D
7.	A	28.	D	49.	A
8.	D	29.	B	50.	D
9.	B	30.	B	51.	C
10.	B	31.	D	52.	A
11.	A	32.	D	53.	C
12.	B	33.	A	54.	A
13.	B	34.	B	55.	D
14.	C	35.	C	56.	C
15.	C	36.	D	57.	D
16.	A	37.	A	58.	B
17.	C	38.	C	59.	A
18.	A	39.	A	60.	B
19.	D	40.	B	61.	B
20.	A	41.	B	62.	A
21.	B	42.	B	63.	D

64. D	88. A	112. B
65. C	89. C	113. B
66. B	90. C	114. D
67. D	91. D	115. B
68. C	92. C	116. A
69. D	93. C	117. A
70. B	94. B	118. D
71. A	95. B	119. C
72. B	96. A	120. D
73. C	97. D	121. A
74. D	98. C	122. B
75. A	99. A	123. B
76. B	100. D	124. C
77. C	101. B	125. D
78. B	102. D	126. B
79. A	103. C	127. A
80. C	104. D	128. D
81. C	105. A	129. B
82. D	106. A	130. C
83. B	107. B	131. A
84. A	108. A	132. C
85. C	109. D	133. A
86. A	110. D	134. C
87. D	111. D	135. C

136. A	160. B	184. B
137. B	161. A	185. A
138. C	162. A	186. D
139. A	163. D	187. C
140. C	164. D	188. B
141. D	165. B	189. A
142. C	166. C	190. D
143. C	167. A	191. D
144. B	168. D	192. A
145. D	169. C	193. C
146. C	170. B	194. B
147. A	171. A	195. D
148. A	172. A	196. B
149. B	173. B	197. A
150. B	174. D	198. C
151. A	175. A	199. A
152. A	176. A	200. B
153. B	177. B	201. C
154. D	178. C	202. B
155. C	179. A	203. D
156. D	180. D	204. A
157. C	181. C	205. B
158. C	182. C	206. C
159. A	183. A	207. D

208. A

209. C

210. B

211. A

212. C

213. D

214. B

215. B

216. B

217. A

218. D

219. B

220. D

221. D

222. B

223. C

224. A

225. B

Answer Explanations

1. **Answer: (C) PERT Chart**
    A Program Evaluation and Review Technique (PERT) chart shows the critical path for a project. The critical path is determined by adding the times for the activities in each sequence and determining the longest path in the project.

2. **Answer: (A) Identifying Threats and Opportunities**
    Although all of the answers seem correct, identifying threats and opportunities is an integral part of strategy development in HR.

3. **Answer: (C) SHRM**
    The Society for Human Resource Management (SHRM) is the largest HR-related organization. It was originally founded as the American Society for Personnel Administration (ASPA) in 1948. You can find additional information about SHRM at www.SHRM.org.

4. **Answer: (D) Supply Chain**
   Human Resources does not commonly provide the role of Supply Chain management. This is a common role of Procurement or Materials Management in an organization.

5. **Answer: (C) Capacity**
   Capacity is defined as the capability to produce.

6. **Answer: (A) A Policy**
   The key is the term 'activities'. Policies address employee and management activities in an organization.

7. **Answer: (A) Recognition by the OFCCP**
   The OFCCP is the Office of Federal Contract Compliance Programs. This office is responsible for ensuring the contractors doing business with Federal government do not discriminate and enforces affirmative action. This agency does not have any relation to defining or approving professions.

8. **Answer: (D) Organizing**
The management function of *organizing* best describes the actions being taken by the HR manager. This management function reflects the organization of HR resources to achieve an HR goal or initiative.

9. **Answer: (B) Human Resource Management Strategy**
HRMS commonly stands for a Human Resource Management System.

10. **Answer: (B) Data Warehouse**
A data warehouse is a large database that stores organizational metrics so they can be retrieved for future analysis. An intranet is an internal web site that employees can use to look up company and employee information. An application service provider is a 3rd party software provider that hosts the software outside of the company. Streaming video is video that can be viewed over the internet.

11. **Answer: (A) Value associated with a brand name**
Brand equity is defined as the commercial value that derives from consumer perception of the brand name of a particular product or company.

12. **Answer: (B) Veto**

The definition of a veto is the rejection of a decision or proposal made by a law-making body.

13. **Answer: (B) Relative approach**

A relative approach measures the company against direct competitors and peers that compete in the same market.

14. **Answer: (C) GANNT Chart**

The GANNT chart is commonly used to show the start and end dates of tasks. The other tools and charts are used for other means.

15. **Answer: (C) Growth**

The organizational life cycle step of *growth* is when the demand for a company's products is greater than the company's ability to meet the demand. This best fits with the scenario described in the question.

16. **Answer: (A) 2/3**

1 standard deviation from the mean is about 34%. If you take 1 standard deviation and take -1 standard deviation that is 34% + 34%. This is 68%. 2/3 of the data will roughly fall within -1 or +1 standard deviations.

17. **Answer: (C) backed up routinely**
Disasters, human errors and viruses can destroy data. It is vital that organizations have a disaster recovery plan regarding the availability and integrity of their data. One key task to ensure this is to routinely back up the data.

18. **Answer: (A) Increase in manual processes**
HR technologies should reduce the need for manual processes so that productivity can be increased and duplicate data entry can be reduced. Automating manual processes using HR technologies can help achieve those goals.

19. **Answer: (D) A virtual organization**
A virtual organization would best fit into an organic organization. Organic organizations are categorized as being flexible and highly adaptive. The other answers are all forms of rigid, highly controlled organizational structures.

20. **Answer: (A) Strategies**
Strategies are not a component of the SWOT analysis. The "S" stands for *Strengths*.

21. **Answer: (B) Benchmarking**
Benchmarking is the process of comparing your data against the data of other organizations. Critical path analysis is a project management tool. Forecasting is used to predict future results. SWOT analysis is used for strategic planning.

22. **Answer: (D) Skills inventory**
A skills inventory is listing of abilities, capacities, qualifications and career goals of the employees of a company. Skills inventories can be used to identify suitable candidates for internal recruitment and promotions.

23. **Answer: (A) Quorum**
A quorum is the minimal number of officers and members of a committee or organization who must be present for a valid transaction of business.

24. **Answer: (B) Assets**
The fundamental accounting equation is used in this question which is "assets = liabilities + owners' equity"

25. **Answer: (D) Is continual**
Projects usually have set deadlines or target dates for completion and are not on-going.

26. **Answer: (C) A snapshot of a company's financial condition**
A balance sheet is a summary of an organization's assets, liabilities and ownership equity as of a specific date. Answer A and B are based on a period of time instead of a specific date in time. Answer D is an example of what you might find on a statement of cash flows.

27. **Answer: (A) Zero-based budgeting**
The example best describes zero-based budgeting. Incremental budgeting uses previous budgets as a starting point. Formula based budgets use a percent based increase or decrease to a previous year's budget. Activity-based budgeting links budgets to a company's goals or initiatives.

28. **Answer: (D) Profit**
The four "P"s are *pricing, promotion, place* and *product*.

29. **Answer: (B) Span of control**
The span of control is defined as the number of subordinates a supervisor has.

30. **Answer: (B) HR audit**
An HR audit is commonly used by organizations to determine the effectiveness of its HR programs. Cost-benefit analysis and return-on-investment are used to aid in decision-making. A SWOT analysis is for environment scanning to help formulate or determine HR strategies.

31. **Answer: (D) Improve unity of command**
Answers A, B and C describe the setup and the advantages of a matrix reporting structure. One of the disadvantages of a matrix structure is that it does not promote a unity of command.

32. **Answer: (D) Data is collected and analyzed but a decision is not made and no action is taken.**
Analysis paralysis occurs when an organization continues to collect data but never makes a decision or takes action.

33. **Answer: (A) Correlation**
Correlation is not considered a measure of central tendency. The mean, mode and median are all considered measures of central tendency.

34. **Answer: (B) 3**
The mean is the average. The average of
$(1+1+3+3+5+5)/6 = 3$.

35. **Answer: (C) Fairly diverse**
If there is a large standard deviation then
this reflects that the data is widely
dispersed from the average value.

36. **Answer: (D) Qualitative analysis**
With qualitative analysis, data collection
methods can include interviews and group
discussions and observation.

37. **Answer: (A) Sandwich generation**
The sandwich generation is the portion of
the baby boomers who are now caring for
both their aging parents and their children.

38. **Answer: (C) Utility patent**
A utility patent is issued for the invention
of a new and useful process, machine,
manufacture, or composition of matter, or
a new and useful improvement thereof, it
generally permits its owner to exclude
others from making, using, or selling the
invention for a period of up to twenty years
from the date of patent application filing.

39. **Answer: (A) Their peers**
Forced ranking is a system where managers
identify their best and worst performers by
comparing them to one another.

40. **Answer: (B) Cause-and-effect diagram**
Another name for the Ishikawa Chart is the Cause-and-Effect diagram. It is also known as the Fishbone Diagram.

41. **Answer: (B) Redesigning jobs**
Redesigning jobs is not considered a human process intervention. The other answers are all examples of human process interventions. Redesigning jobs is considered a technostructural intervention.

42. **Answer: (B) Vague**
When defining an objective for an employee, it should not be vague. It should be measurable, reasonable and timely.

43. **Answer: (D) Problem identification**
The steps in the scientific method are:

1. Problem identification/analysis
2. Hypothesis development
3. Research design
4. Data collection
5. Data analysis

44. **Answer: (A) Construct validity**
Construct validity helps determine if the measurement actually measures something that cannot be observed. Content validity measures the extent that the measure is what was intended to be measured. Concurrent and predictive validity fall under criterion-related validity that predicts future performance.

45. **Answer: (B) If data is valid, it must be reliable**
For data to be valid, it must also be reliable.

46. **Answer: (A) 2**
The *mode* is the number that occurs the most frequently in a set of numbers.

47. **Answer: (B) 5**
The *median* is the number that divides the distribution of the numbers in half.

48. **Answer: (D) 99%**
99.74% of all values will be located within 3 standard deviations from the mean.

49. **Answer: (A) As the value of one measure decreases, the other measure increases.**
If there is a relationship where the value of X decreases as Y increases, then a negative correlation exists. In the example of X decreases as Y decreases or X increases as Y increases, this shows a positive correlation.

50. **Answer: (D) All are components of an effective ethics program.**
All of the examples given are components commonly found in effective ethic programs.

51. **Answer: (C) 15**
According to www.eeoc.gov, a company must have at least 15 employees to fall under Title VII of the Civil Rights Act.

52. **Answer: (A) OFCCP**
The Office of Federal Contract Compliance Programs is the government agency that enforces the requirements of affirmative action.

53. **Answer: (C) 40**
The Age Discrimination in Employment Act of 1967 (ADEA) protects individuals who are 40 years of age or older from employment discrimination based on age.

54. **Answer: (A) Pregnancy-related benefits are limited to married employees.**
The EEOC specifies that pregnancy-related benefits CANNOT be limited to married employees. All of the other answers are provisions under the Pregnancy Discrimination Act.

55. **Answer: (D) 72**
An employee must complete an I-9 form within 72 hours of employment.

56. **Answer: (C) 400 full-time, 100 part-time employee will be laid off**
Part-time employee are excluded from the WARN Act calculations to determine if the 60 day notice is required. With answer C, there must be at least 500 full-time employees to constitute the notice.

57. **Answer: (D) Individuals currently engaging in the illegal use of drugs**
Employees and applicants currently engaging in the illegal use of drugs are not covered by the ADA.

58. **Answer: (B) Age**
Title VII covers race, color, religion, or national origin. It does not cover age discrimination. That is protected by the Age Discrimination in Employment Act (ADEA).

59. **Answer: (A) Griggs v. Duke Power**
Griggs v. Duke Power established the judicial concept of adverse impact (also referred to as disparate impact). Adverse impact is defined as a "theory of liability that prohibits an employer from using a facially neutral employment practice that has an unjustified adverse impact on members of a protected class".

60. **Answer: (B) It does not provide an incentive for the employee to produce at a high level**
"Piecework" provides higher motivation to produce at a high level since employees are paid based on their productivity.

61. **Answer: (B) McDonnell-Douglas Corp. v. Green**

    Since the McDonnell-Douglas Corp. v. Green ruling, all of the federal courts have subsequently adopted the order and allocation of proof set out for all claims of disparate-treatment employment discrimination that are not based on direct evidence of discriminatory intent.

62. **Answer: (A) A polygraph test can be performed because the employee is a suspect and a loss was realized**

    Under the Polygraph Protection Act of 1988 (EPPA) a polygraph test can be performed on a suspect when a loss is realized by a company.

63. **Answer: (D) Albermarle Paper Company v. Moody**

    The Albermarle Paper Company v. Moody ruling determined the requirements placed upon an employer to establish that pre-employment tests have a discriminatory effect are sufficiently "job related" to survive a legal challenge.

64. **Answer: (D) Is required to pay the employee the bonus when they return**

Under the Family Medical Leave Act, an employer is required to treat employees on leave the same as current active employees. In this scenario, the employer must pay the employee the full bonus during their leave or upon their return.

65. **Answer: (C) UGESP**

For this question, it is helpful to know what these common HR acronyms stand for. SOX stands for the Sarbanes-Oxley Act. HIPAA stands for the Health Insurance Portability and Accountability Act. ADEA is short for the Age Discrimination in Employment Act. The correct answer is UGESP which stands for Uniform Guidelines on Employee Selection Procedures. For the actual exam, you should be familiar with all of these terms.

66. **Answer: (B) Comparing the availability analysis with the job group analysis**
The utilization analysis is prepared after availability rates for minorities and women in each job group are established. The percentage of minorities and women participating in each job group is compared with the availability of minorities and women in each job group. Any job group where the current participation rate is lower than the availability rate by one whole person is identified as underutilized.

67. **Answer: (D) 80%**
Adverse impact occurs when the rate of selection for a protected class is less than 80% of the rate for the class with the highest selection rate.

68. **Answer: (C) Continue with the procedure**
If adverse impact is identified, an HR manager should not continue with the procedure. He or she should use the other options provided by the alternative answers.

69. **Answer: (D) Internal availability and external availability**
The two factors of the "two-factor analysis" under affirmative action are *internal availability* and *external availability*.

70. **Answer: (B) Employee's mother-in-law**
Employees have the right to take leave only to care for someone who is a biological or adoptive parent.

71. **Answer: (A) Adverse impact**
The example best describes the occurrence of adverse impact.

72. **Answer: (B) Express oral contract**
This scenario described in the question is an example of an express oral contract.

73. **Answer: (C) The time the employee was waiting is not considered hours worked**
According to the Portal-to-Portal Act, the time an employee waits on the worksite before their scheduled time is not considered hours worked.

74. **Answer: (D) Commuting time is not paid work time regardless of the employee using a company vehicle or not**
As defined by the Act, commuting time is never considered paid work time regardless of an employee using a company vehicle or not.

75. **Answer: (A) Equal Pay Act**
The Equal Pay Act was an amendment to the Wage and Hour Law which prohibits unequal pay between men and women for "substantially equal" work.

76. **Answer: (B) Seniority**
Seniority is not considered when determining equal work factors. All of the other answers are used to determine equal work factors.

77. **Answer: (C) Worker Relocation Tax Credit**
All of the answers offer special tax credits to employers who hire certain individuals except for the "Worker Relocation Tax Credit".

78. **Answer: (B) Regent of the University of California v. Bakke**

In the court ruling of Regents of the University of California v. Bakke, the court ruled 5-4 in Bakke's favor. The court opinion stated that race could be only one of numerous factors used by discriminatory boards, such as those of college admissions. The court found that quotas insulated minority applicants from competition with the regular applicants and were thus unconstitutional because they discriminated against non-minority applicants

79. **Answer: (A) Quid pro quo**

This is an example of a *quid pro quo* (Latin for *this for that*). *Carpe diem* is Latin for seize the day. *Caveat emptor* is Latin for *let the buyer beware. Per diem* is Latin for *through a day.*

80. **Answer: (C) Glass ceiling**

A glass ceiling refers to the prevention of a promotion based on discrimination.

81. **Answer: (C) The EEOC determines if it has jurisdiction over the complaint filed**
The EEOC must determine if it has jurisdiction over the compliant before it takes any other actions.

82. **Answer: (D) Delphi technique**
One of the specifications of the Delphi technique is that the participants never actually meet face-to-face. The general methodology is for a group of experts to independently develop and refine forecasts until a group consensus is met.

83. **Answer: (B) Replacement charting**
Although succession planning and replacement charting are very similar, replacement charting looks at the readiness of current employees and their readiness to step into leadership positions. Succession planning is a long-term strategy for developing candidates to fill future job openings.

84. **Answer: (A) Questionnaires and checklists**

If there are a large number of employees doing the same job that are spread out over a wide geographic area then questionnaires and checklists would be the most appropriate method to collect the data. Observation and work sampling is difficult to accomplish with a large number of employees especially if they are spread out geographically. Interviews would also be difficult, time-consuming and costly based on the large number of employees and the geographic separation.

85. **Answer: (C) Working conditions**

The work environment and conditions are typically found in the *working conditions* section of the job description. The job summary is a summary of the job, the essential functions describe the functions of the job and the qualifications section lists required or preferred qualifications to perform the job.

86. **Answer: (A) Brings new ideas into the workplace**

Answers B, C and D are typical advantages of hiring from within. Although A could be true of hiring from within, the likelihood of bringing in new and fresh ideas with an external employee is higher.

87. **Answer: (D) Assessment Center Tests**

Assessment center tests are complex and usually have multiple raters. Assessment center testing is a large investment for an organization and can be very costly. Because of this, it is commonly used for the selection and development of high-level positions.

88. **Answer: (A) Recruitment is more difficult**

When unemployment levels are low, the external candidate pool to select from is usually much smaller. This can make recruitment more difficult.

89. **Answer: (C) Situational interview**
A situational interview is one in which the recruiter asks a candidate how they act in certain situations. Situational interview questions could be asked in a structured or informal interview but other types of questions could be asked as well. In a stress interview, the candidate is placed under pressure or anxiety to see how they would respond under those conditions.

90. **Answer: (C) EO 11246**
Executive Order 11246 prohibited employment discrimination on the basis of race, creed, color or national origin.

91. **Answer: (D) Have you worked at this company before?**
Answers A, B, C are not appropriate questions for an interview (unless there is a specific BFOQ that would allow the question).

92. **Answer: (C) 3 years**
You should retain payroll records for at least 3 years.

93. **Answer: (C) Whether permission was obtained from the copyright owner**
The fair use rule is used to determine if a copyright violation has occurred when the permission of the copyright owner was not obtained. If the permission of the copyright owner was obtained, then the fair use test does not need to be used. This is a bit of a trick question but you can expect a couple of vague, tricky questions on the exam as well.

94. **Answer: (B) Andragogy**
The correct term coined by Malcolm Knowles that describe adult learning is *andragogy*.

95. **Answer: (B) Auditory**
The scenario described in the question is an example of someone who learns through auditory interactions.

96. **Answer: (A) Synthesis**
Synthesis is the level of learning that is achieved when a learner is able to take information from multiple sources and create new meaning by reaching a conclusion based on that information. The other levels of learning must be achieved before synthesis can be achieved.

97. **Answer: (D) Motivation**
Although motivation can be a characteristic that fits into one of the five needs, it is not explicitly defined as one of the five needs.

98. **Answer: (C) Employees are self-motivated**
Employees are self motivated belongs to the Theory Y list.

99. **Answer: (A) Hygiene**
Hygiene and motivation are the two factors of the Herzberg theory. The other answers belong to Maslow's hierarchy of need.

100. **Answer: (D) Culture**
Unfreezing, movement, and refreezing are all components of the model. Culture is not a component.

101. **Answer: (B) Expectancy theory**
The expectancy theory's basic premise is that effort will lead to a positive outcome. There is substantial research that supports this theory which shows a linkage between compensation and performance. Goal theory postulates that motivation increases when goals are set. Herzberg's theory focuses on motivation and hygiene. McClelland's theory states that motivation is based on the need for achievement, power and affiliation.

102. **Answer: (D) Visual**
PowerPoint is a slideshow technology where information is displayed on a projected screen. This best fits with the visual learning style.

103. **Answer: (C) Program Initiation**
ADDIE stands for Needs Assessment, Program Design, Program Development, Program Implementation and Program Evaluation.

104. **Answer: (D) Role-playing**
Role-playing best describes this scenario. None of the other delivery methods have the learner act out a pretend scenario.

105. **Answer: (A) Banquet**
Banquet-style seating breaks the participants up into small groups. This arrangement would best accommodate the need for breakout sessions and group activities.

106. **Answer: (A) Management by Objectives (MBO)**
Management by Objectives is a process of defining objectives within an organization so that management and employees agree to the organization's goals and understand what they need to do to achieve them.

107. **Answer: (B) The employee did not violate any copyright protections of the document because government documents are considered public domain**
All government web site information is considered public domain and can be used without the concern of violating a copyright protection.

108. **Answer: (A) Reception**
The four levels are reaction, learning, behavior and results.

109. **Answer: (D) Transactional leadership**
The manager in this example is exhibiting the characteristics of a transactional leader.

110. **Answer: (D) Tradition**
Tradition is a set of customs or practices. Unless those customs or practices are changing, then they are not usually a driving force that brings about change. The other answers are all examples of a driving force that brings about change.

111. **Answer: (D) Behavior**
Only two of the four answers are a level in Kirkpatrick's model. The level of behavior is when an employee takes information learned and applies it on-the-job.

112. **Answer: (B) Pareto**
The Pareto chart shows the cumulative percentage of events and provides an analysis based on the theory that 80 percent of the problems are caused by 20 percent of the reasons. GANTT and PERT charts are project management tools. The histogram graphs similar information but does not include the cumulative percentage.

113. **Answer: (B) Dual career ladder**
Dual career ladders allow employees to choose a path between being a technical expert and moving into a leadership role. Matrix is an organization structure. Job bidding and succession plans do not usually accommodate this scenario.

114. **Answer: (D) Visionary**
This is an example of visionary leadership. Be sure to be familiar with all four of the leadership styles shown in the answers.

115. **Answer: (B) Individual level training**
The five characteristics of a learning organization are systems-thinking, personal mastery, mental models, building a shared vision and team learning.

116. **Answer: (A) Ranking**
The four types of learning evaluation are reaction, learning, behavior and results.

117. **Answer: (A) Identification of the performance gap**
The first step in conducting a training needs analysis is to identify the goal, the current level of training and the performance gap.

118. **Answer: (D) 9,9**
The most favorable spot to be on in the managerial grid is the top-right cell (9,9). This demonstrates the highest level of concern for people and concern for production.

119. **Answer: (C) Employee's peers may give higher or lower ratings based on non-work related item**
All of the examples are advantages of peer-team ratings except C. C is a potential disadvantage of the peer-team rating model.

120. **Answer: (D) Contrast error**
Contrast error is when a manager rates an employee based on the performance of other employees.

121. **Answer: (A) Uniform Guidelines on Employee Selection Procedures**
The Uniform Guidelines of Employee Selection Procedures is a comprehensive document regarding the legality of employee selection procedures. It does not have a direct impact on the compensation or benefits of an employee.

122. **Answer: (B) Paid Time Off**
The Fair Labor Standards Act does not cover paid time off. It does cover answers A, C and D.

123. **Answer: (B) 12**
The Family and Medical Leave Act grants an employee 12 weeks of unpaid medical leave.

124. **Answer: (C) 30 days**
Under the Family and Medical Leave Act, an employee must give 30 days notice if the leave can be reasonably anticipated.

125. **Answer: (D) Omnibus Budget Reconciliation Act**
The Omnibus Budget Reconciliation Act has this requirement included within it.

126. **Answer: (B) Whether someone is an employee or an independent contractor**
The IRS 20-Factor Test is used to determine whether someone is an employee or an independent contractor. You can find additional information on the U.S. Chamber of Commerce Small Business Center web site.

127. **Answer: (A) Ranking**
This is an example of ranking jobs. The *paired comparison* methods is where you take all of the jobs and create a matrix of them listing them across the vertical and horizontal axis. You then compare each job to every other job.

128. **Answer: (D) Factor comparison**
Of all of the job evaluation methods listed, *factor comparison* is the one that uses compensable factors and external job market benchmarks. With the point factor model, the jobs are placed within a hierarchy of pay grades. Ranking is taking all of the jobs and ranking from most to least important. Job classification does not rely on compensable factors.

129. **Answer: (B) Broad-banding**
Broad-banding is the when multiple pay grades are collapsed into one broad pay grade. This allows for flexibility, efficiency, decentralization and a focus on performance.

130. **Answer: (C) Pay compression**
The scenario described in the question commonly causes pay compression which occurs when the pay rates for skilled employees with experience are not much higher than newly hired employees.

131. **Answer: (A) Red circle rate was identified**
A red circle rate is identified when an employee's pay rate is over the maximum of their pay grade. A green circle is when the pay rate is below the minimum pay rate for the grade.

132. **Answer: (C) Employee Retirement Income Security Act (ERISA)**
This is a requirement defined by ERISA.

133. **Answer: (A) Piece rate plan**
A piece rate plan pays an employee based on their production output. B and C do not pay more based on a higher level of output.

134. **Answer: (C) Base pay**
Hazard pay, shift pay and overtime are all differentials. Base pay is the foundation of an employer's compensation program.

135. **Answer: (C) Recognizes superior individual performance**
All of the answers are potential advantages of company-wide incentives except for C. One of the side effects of organization-wide incentives is that superior individual performance may be overlooked.

136. **Answer: (A) Generous severance plan for executives**
Golden parachutes are contractual agreements that guarantee that an executive will receive a predetermined amount of money if terminated from the organization.

137. **Answer: (B) Intrinsic reward**
An intrinsic reward is a reward that comes from the inside. Feelings of satisfaction for completing a project is an example of an intrinsic reward. A compensatory reward is a type of an extrinsic reward. "Total Rewards" is a term used to describe a company's pay and benefits package.

138. **Answer: (C) Knowledge, skills and abilities**
KSA stands for *knowledge, skills and abilities*. These are the unique requirements that help determine the best person to fulfill the needs of a particular job.

139. **Answer: (A) Qualified Domestic Relations Orders**
QDRO stands for Qualified Domestic Relations Orders. A QDRO is a legal order subsequent to a divorce or legal separation that splits and changes ownership of a retirement plan to give the divorced spouse their share of the asset or pension plan.

140. **Answer: (C) Fair Labor Standards Act (FLSA)**
All of the acts listed directly apply to a company's cash balance pension plan except for the Fair Labor Standards Act. The Fair Labor Standards Act applies to employee wage and hours.

141. **Answer: (D) Consumer Credit Protection Act (CCPA)**
The Consumer Credit Protection Act (CCPA) protects an employee from being terminated solely based on the fact that their wages are being garnished for a single debt.

142. **Answer: (C) Job specifications**
These types of qualifications fall under the job specification category. Essential job functions describe the key tasks performed on the job. Competencies are specific skills that an employee must have. Job enrichment is a way to motivate employees by giving them opportunities to use their abilities.

143. **Answer: (C) EB-1**
The only answer that is an immigrant visa is an EB-1.

144. **Answer: (B) Non-exempt status**
All of the answers are examples of executive perks except for having non-exempt status. Exempt status is used to determine if the organization must pay an employee overtime or not.

145. **Answer: (D) Bereavement**
Currently, bereavement (funeral leave) is not a federally mandated benefit that employers must offer.

146. **Answer: (C) Fee-for-service plans**
Fee-for-service provides the most flexibility. The other plans usually incentivize employees for using recommended service providers.

147. **Answer: (A) Offering a robust severance package**
Severance packages are offered to terminated employees. Once an employee has been terminated, their work/life balance with regards to recent employment is no longer the issue.

148. **Answer: (A) Section 125**
Section 125 of the tax code permits this type of tax benefit to employees.

149. **Answer: (B) The employee forfeits any unspent funds**
Flexible spending accounts fall under "use it or lose it". Any unused funds are forfeited by the employee.

150. **Answer: (B) 1**
Comp-ratio is defined as the employee's pay rate over the mid-point of grade. In this scenario, the employee's comp-ratio is 1.

151. **Answer: (A) That the Wagner Act was constitutional**
This particular Supreme Court case established that the Wagner act was indeed constitutional.

152. **Answer: (A) American Federation of Labor**
The American Federation of Labor was one of the first national unions. The Knights of Labor is another example.

153. **Answer: (B) Constructive discharge**
When a manager makes an environment that is hostile or inhospitable in an attempt to get an employee to leave, this is an example of constructive discharge.

154. **Answer: (D) Paid time off**
Social Security, Medicare, unemployment insurance, COBRA and FMLA are all mandatory benefits. Paid time off is not a benefit mandated by a federal statute.

155. **Answer: (C) Salary survey**
A salary survey is a tool used to determine the current market trends and an analysis of pay for different knowledge and skills within different markets.

156. **Answer: (D) $7.25**
The federal minimum wage as of 7/24/2009 is $7.25.

157. **Answer: (C) Fair Labor Standards Act (FLSA)**
The federal minimum wage was established by the FLSA.

158. **Answer: (C) The teen works 20 hours per week when school is in session**
A 15-year-old can only work 18 hours or less a week while school is in session.   All of the other answers are legal.

159. **Answer: (A) Issuing a statement to all employees that the company is not in favor of being unionized**
Companies have a legal right to distribute factual information and share their companies opinion regarding unions so that employees can make an informed decision.

160. **Answer: (B) A yellow-dog contract**
A yellow-dog contract is when an employer makes someone agree not to join a union as a condition of their employment.

161. **Answer: (A) Norris-LaGuardia Act**
In 1932, the Norris-LaGuardia Act outlawed yellow-dog contracts which are where an employer forces a person to agree not to join a union as a condition of their employment.

162. **Answer: (A) Salting**
Salting is a labor union tactic involving the act of getting a job at a specific company with the intent of organizing a union.

163. **Answer: (D) Labor Management Reporting and Disclosure Act**
The official name of the Landrum-Griffin Act is the Labor Management Reporting and Disclosure Act.

164. **Answer: (D) Excelsior List**
The question clearly defines what an Excelsior list contains.

165. **Answer: (B) Circuit City v. Adams**
In 2001, the Supreme Court's decision was that compulsory arbitration as a condition of employment is legal.

166. **Answer: (C) Employees**
Mangers, supervisors, confidential employees and several others are not allowed in a bargaining unit. Although the term employees is vague and could mean many different things, it is the MOST acceptable answer given the other answers.

167. **Answer: (A) Salting**
Salting, where a union tries to get a union member hired into the organization to help organize the union efforts, is a permissible tactic.

168. **Answer: (D) Put a non-solicitation policy in place**
Employers cannot do any of the other answers but they can put a non-solicitation policy in place.

169. **Answer: (C) 30%**
30% of the bargaining unit must sign the decertification petition.

170. **Answer: (B) Shift differential pay**
All of the answers are mandatory bargaining items except for shift differential pay.

171. **Answer: (A) Permissive bargaining item**
A permission bargaining item is an item in which both parties agree to bargain on which is not a mandatory bargaining item.

172. **Answer: (A) Illegal bargaining item**
Closed shops are not legal and cannot be used in the collective bargaining process. This is an example of an illegal bargaining item.

173. **Answer: (B) 30%**
The NLRB will hold an election after 30% of authorization cards have been signed by the bargaining unit.

174. **Answer: (D) Statutory bar**
This is an example of a statutory bar.

175. **Answer: (A) 6 months**
In this example, the union must wait 6 months.

176. **Answer: (A) Agency shop**
A union shop is one in which employees must pay union dues whether they are a member of the union or not.

177. **Answer: (B) Closed shop**
Closed shop clauses are illegal (except in construction).

178. **Answer: (C) Zipper clause**
Zipper clauses help to prevent this from happening.

179. **Answer: (A) Strike**
A strike is a temporary stoppage of work initiated by a group of employees working at an organization.

180. **Answer: (D) Closed Shop**
A closed shop is not a common bargaining tactic because it is illegal. The other answers are common bargaining tactics taken by employees.

181. **Answer: (C) Corporate compaign**
The scenario described best reflects a corporate campaign. A boycott is when a group of customers refuse to buy the company's products. A picket line is a group of employee who walk in front of the company with signs. An agency shop is when non-union employees have to pay union dues.

182. **Answer: (C) Double breasted**
Double breasting is a company that has both union and non-union subsidiaries.

183. **Answer: (A) Common situs**
Common situs picketing is described as picketing by a labor union of an entire construction project as a result of a grievance held against a single subcontractor on the project.

184. **Answer: (B) Lockout**
A lockout is when an employer prevents workers from working is a tactic used by a company's management. The other answers are common tactics used by the labor union, not the employer.

185. **Answer: (A) When future bargaining will not likely result in an agreement**
Impasse is when a likely agreement is not expected between the union and organization.

186. **Answer: (D) Agency shop**
All of the answers are common contract provisions. And although answer D) is a union security clause it is illegal in right-to-work states which make it the least common.

187. **Answer: (C) An arbitrator selected by the government**
A three-person arbitration panel typically consist of an arbitrator selected by the company, by the union and a joint, neutral arbitrator.

188. **Answer: (B) Wildcat strike**
The scenario describes a wildcat strike.

189. **Answer: (A) Sympathy strike**
This is an example of a sympathy strike.

190. **Answer: (D) Appeal/enforcement**
The steps of an NLRB unfair labor practice complaint are initiation, investigation, hearing, cease and desist order and finally the appeal/enforcement process.

191. **Answer: (D) Federal Labor Relations Authority (FLRA)**
The Federal Labor Relations Authority (FLRA) has similar responsibilities to the NLRA except that it is over federal employees.

192. **Answer: (A) NAFTA**
NAFTA stands for the North American Free Trade Agreement between the United States, Canada and Mexico.

193. **Answer: (C) Employment-at-will**
Employment-at-will allows an employee or employer to end the employment agreement at any time for any reason.

194. **Answer: (B) Employment contract**
Although breaking an employment contract can result in a tort, a wrongful act that harms a person and is actionable in court, it is not in itself a tort. The other answers could fall under a tort.

195. **Answer: (D) Termination**
Termination is the final step in the progressive disciplinary process.

196. **Answer: (B) Ombudsman**
The scenario described in the question fits the description of an ombudsman.

197. **Answer: (A) Lean**
A "lean" process is one in which many of its unnecessary steps have been removed.

198. **Answer: (C) 12 months**
A union must wait 12 months before they can hold another election.

199. **Answer: (A) Sherman Antitrust Act**
The Sherman Antitrust Act created July 2, 1890, requires the United States Federal government to investigate potential cartels and monopolies.

200. **Answer: (B) Clayton Act**
The Clayton Act of 1914 was implemented to prevent anticompetitive practices. It established that injunctions could only be used when property damage was threatened.

201. **Answer: (C) Hot-cargo clause**
The scenario described in the question describes a hot-cargo clause which is when union members refuse to handle goods made by another non-union plant.

202. **Answer: (B) Occupational Safety and Health Act**
The Occupational Safety and Health Administration (OSHA) was established by the Occupational Safety and Health Act.

203. **Answer: (D) Employee Right-to-Know law**
    "Right to know", in the context of United States workplace and community environmental law, is the legal principle that the individual has the right to know the chemicals to which they may be exposed in their daily living.

204. **Answer: (A) Material Safety Data Sheets (MSDS)**
    MSDS stands for Material Safety Data Sheets.

205. **Answer: (B) Lockout**
    The term referred to in the question is most commonly referred to as Lockout.

206. **Answer: (C) Tagout**
    "Lock and tag" works in conjunction with a lock usually locking the device and placing it in such a position that no hazardous power sources can be turned on. The procedure requires that a tag be affixed to the locked device indicating that it should not be turned on. Also known as tagout.

207. **Answer: (D) Bloodborne Pathogens standard**
    The Needlestick Safety and Prevention Act revised the Bloodborne Pathogen standard.

208. **Answer: (A) Fellow servant rule**
The *fellow servant rule* absolves employers of responsibility if a coworker's actions cause an injury.

209. **Answer: (C) The general duty standard**
Also known as the 'unholy trinity', the three common law doctrines that apply to workers injured on the job are the fellow servant rule, the doctrine of contributory negligence and the voluntary assumption of risk. The general duty standard requires employers to provide jobs and a workplace environment that are free from recognized safety and health hazards.

210. **Answer: (B) 10**
Companies with 10 or more employees must report employee occupational injuries and illnesses.

211. **Answer: (A) MSDS documentation is provided to employees**
All of the answers apply to the OSHA Confined Space Entry standard except the need to have MSDS documentation. MSDS communication is required by the Hazard Communication standard.

212. **Answer: (C) First aid-treatment**
Days away from work, loss of consciousness and death must be reported under OSHA. First aid-treatment under most circumstances does not.

213. **Answer: (D) OSHA Form 300**
OSHA Form 300 is the appropriate form to use in this scenario. Be sure to be aware of the differences between the other OSHA forms.

214. **Answer: (B) OSHA Form 300A**
OSHA Form 300a is the appropriate form to use in this scenario. Be sure to be aware of the differences between the other OSHA forms.

215. **Answer: (B) 7 days**
The OSHA Form 301 must be completed within 7 days of finding out about a work-related injury or illness.

216. **Answer: (B) Days away, restricted or transferred**
DART stands for "days away, restricted or transferred".

217. **Answer: (A) No notice**
An OSHA compliance and safety officer does not have to give any notice before showing up to a work site.

218. **Answer: (D) Be given 48 hours notice before the compliance officer can perform the inspection**
As described in the previous answer, a compliance officer does not have to give any notice before showing up on site.

219. **Answer: (B) De Minimis**
This would be considered a "de minimis" violation.

220. **Answer: (D) Willful**
This would be considered a "willful" violation.

221. **Answer: (D) Three days or until the violation is corrected, whichever is longer**
The violation must be posted at the site of the violation for three days or until the violation is corrected, whichever is longer.

222. **Answer: (B) Heavy lifting**
Although heavy lifting can be a cause of a musculoskeletal disorder, the more common causes are frequent repetitions, excessive pressure and awkward positions over a lengthy duration of time.

223. **Answer: (C) An unsafe act**
Lack of or improper use of Protective Personal Equipment falls under the category of an unsafe act. An unsafe condition is a condition in the work place that is likely to cause injury. A willful violation is a level of violation defined by OSHA.

224. **Answer: (A) National Institute for Occupational Safety and Health**
Employers should contact the National Institute for Occupational Safety and Health (NIOSH) for information regarding substances that may be toxic.

225. **Answer: (B) Willful**
A willful violation is defined as being intentional or known and receives a maximum penalty of up to $70,000. A repeat violation can have a fine of up to $70,000 as well but is defined as being a continued violation.

For additional online practice tests, be sure to visit

www.PHRprep.com.